ELISABETH WETZLAR

GRACIOUS ROOMS –
COUNTRY STYLE

ELISABETH WETZLAR

GRACIOUS ROOMS –
COUNTRY STYLE

ELISABETH WETZLAR

Gracious Rooms— Country Style

GEORGE G. HARRAP & CO. LTD.

Credits

Index of architects

First published in Great Britain 1970
by George G. Harrap & Co. Ltd
182 High Holborn, London, W.C. 1

© **Verlag Ernst Wasmuth Tübingen** 1970
English Translation © George G. Harrap & Co. Ltd. 1970
SBN 245 59935 5
Printed in Germany

1. COUNTRY ROOMS

A 'country' or 'rustic' room takes many forms. The term 'country style' ranges from the farmhouse room to the interior created by all the newly developed materials and principles of construction.

The origin of all country rooms is the farmhouse room. Its characteristics – wooden ceiling, wooden floor, wood-panelled and whitewashed walls – are even today the things which make a room look countrified, even if these elements are translated into different forms and have been replaced and supplemented by new means of construction and design.

The dimensions of the farmhouse rooms were determined by the method of building and the wooden construction of the ceilings: design and furnishing were suited to the requirements of the occupants and were carried out by the local craftsman with wood or other materials from the respective areas.

The prerequisites have changed and different methods of construction make different room dimensions possible. The provision of materials has also become more widespread and various. Today we still endeavour to create a pleasant domestic atmosphere by using the means of design which made the old farmhouse room a particularly cozy place in which to live.

2. OLD FARMHOUSE ROOMS

In our villages nowadays one rarely comes across farmhouse rooms which have lasted for centuries and have been lived in by many generations as the centre of family life.

The attempt to 'modernise' has been too great – particularly in the last fifty years – and unfortunately much that is beautiful and has lasted for centuries has been exchanged in the process for something fleetingly modernistic.

Dealers in rural household furniture knew that their greatest success was to be had when there was a young farmer's wife on the premises; the sturdy chair with the elaborately carved back or arms would be quickly exchanged for something padded and more comfortable, or the painted farmhouse cupboard would be replaced by a complete bedroom suite with a four-door wardrobe, which would be old-fashioned again five years later. Since then the farmhouse room and rural household furniture have been almost completely sold out. There is only a small number of farmers left who have retained their ancestors' sense of heritage and who are prepared to renounce some degree of comfort for the sake of tradition.

On the other hand there are a number of lovers of farmhouse furniture who have found a delight in rural household effects or country-style fittings by natural inclination rather than through having grown up with them; often they are artists, painters, writers, or architects, who value this quite 'unrepresentative' style of interior decoration.

The most beautiful farmhouse rooms and furniture are to be found today in museums. Among these we would especially note the Bavarian National Museum, Munich, the Tyrolese Volks Art Museum, Innsbruck, the Merchant's House in Bessone, Ticino, the Musée des Beaux Arts, Tours, and the Geffrye Museum in Shoreditch, London, where anyone interested can find a comprehensive collection of rural art, and the expert can find a profusion of designs and details of craftsmanship which still retain their validity today.

That typical farmhouse room, always of the same size and built in the same style, which was to be found in every farmhouse, was not restricted to the Southern German area. The large room was on the ground floor, next to the entrance and the kitchen. The smaller room was usually square, with a low timbered ceiling and small windows which were often contained in deep wall openings, and it was heated by a stone or tiled stove. The standard furniture comprised table and chairs in one corner of the room; the corner bench was often extended along the whole wall or was joined to the bench surrounding the stove.

A structural feature of every farmhouse, whether it was made of stone, half-timbering, or wood, was the wood-panelled ceiling, and the longest possible rafter made room dimensions of from 5×5 to 6×6 metres feasible. There were thick joists above the rafters which ran vertically to the top ridge of the roof. Later these ceiling constructions, which were originally visible, were plastered over. Museums have, as show-pieces of rural craftsmanship, farmhouse rooms which have wooden wall panelling, elaborately carved or painted, as well as wooden ceilings. To us, the construction of walls in wood is particularly homely and typical of the concept of 'country-style living', but in practice they were not as common as plastered or whitewashed walls.

3. GRACIOUS ROOMS – COUNTRY STYLE

Many separate pieces of farmhouse furniture have been preserved. They consist mainly of wardrobes, trunks, chests of drawers, beds, and chairs, which belonged upstairs in the farmhouse.

But there are so many lovers of this fine rural household furniture that most of the pieces have found their way from the farmhouse to the towns; so much so that nowadays it is very difficult to discover a really beautiful piece of furniture in the antique markets.

Whether they are made from plain wood either carved or painted, pieces of farmhouse furniture fit well even into an otherwise modern establishment; the wood-coloured painting lends warmth and a personal atmosphere to rooms which are easily made uniform by mass production. Unlike those showpieces of furniture which were made for castles and palaces, one can feel at ease amongst pieces of farmhouse furniture; the rooms for which they were originally built were not so very different in dimension from those of today. And it is not only in proportion and design that they are suited to today's living needs, for they were always planned purposefully and practically; the fact that they were made of wood and that their construction was suited to the materials means that they are both solid and durable.

Whilst pieces of farmhouse furniture were generally made from untreated wood – such as oak, walnut, cherry, larch, fir, and pinewood – which would be provided by a local carpenter, the furniture made from soft wood in the South German area was almost exclusively painted; thus arose a charming variant of the rural style which was entirely dependent upon region.

The succession of great styles which has taken place in the history of art, and which was also to be seen in the art of making furniture, has scarcely affected rural art, and then only indirectly and much later.

The elements of the Gothic style, of Renaissance, Baroque, Rococo, and Empire, were not simply taken over and reproduced in simpler materials, but were adapted by individual ideas and transmuted into folk art; thereby an independent creative mode of craftsmanship came about. Even if the strength of design, which created new tendencies and produced the great styles in the art of furniture making, was missing, it must be realised that, measured by different standards, the delightful products of a naïve inventiveness are still masterpieces of form and colour.

The influence of the Baroque and Rococo styles, on the South German painted cupboards for example, is clearly recognisable and typical of this transference into folk art. The result was an entirely new movement in the painting of furniture; colouring became lighter, painting broke away from structural limitations and went beyond the units delimited by framework and panelling.

Through the influence of Classicism and Empire both shape and modes of painting became plainer and rougher.

In addition to the influence of these styles of art, regional characteristics are what give folk art its character.

Certain artistic modes of expression lasted for centuries in many areas; typical examples are the furniture of the Alpachtal in the Tyrol with its black lead paintwork on shiny wood, or the farmhouse-styled cupboards of Tolz which for long periods were made with the same shaping and style of painting – mostly floral motifs on a dark blue or dark green ground.

Folk art is for the most part anonymous, but with good pieces of furniture, even when one does not know the name of the maker, one feels one can detect the mark of a definite personality. There seems to be some affinity with the South German churches and monasteries of the rural Baroque style, whether it be Wies, Steinhausen, or Zwiefalten. Craftsmen produced great art here too, but without considering themselves to be 'artists'.

It is clear that the creative inventiveness and the artisan's ability of the master craftsmen who designed the churches and monasteries also had an indirect effect upon commercial household furniture.

Individual painters and workshops are known to us by name, such as Johann Michael Rössler from Untermünkheim/Kocher, who often inscribed his name on the front of his cupboards, next to his original motifs (human figures and animals painted in a simple style, or rural flowers); or Franz Baier, who belonged to a family of carpenters and painters in Mudau/Odenwald. Such strong artistic personalities greatly influenced the other workshops in their area; as well as the cupboards originating from Rössler's workshop, a large number of similar pieces of furniture made by contemporary imitators have been preserved in the Schwäbisch-Hall region. Amongst all the regional variety in the choice of colours for painted furniture in the farmhouse style, a predilection for red and blue, the so-called 'country colours', is clearly recognisable, as is a predilection for the motif of flowers in all their diversity, just as they were to be found in the farmhouse gardens. Within the limits of this book we endeavour to show examples of and ideas for modern country rooms.

4. MODERN COUNTRY ROOMS

First of all there is the possibility of fitting single pieces of old farmhouse furniture into an otherwise modern setting. If this synthesis of the old and the new is to be successful, one cannot simply combine the two indiscriminately; but if the antique piece and the modern setting are basically of the same character – suited to the purpose, both appropriate to their material, and made with craftsmanship – scarcely any difficulties would be encountered.

A piece of unpainted wooden furniture makes even fewer demands than

1 Simply painted portraits of the owners and
rustic flowers are characteristic of cupboards by
Johann Michael Rössler. 1824.

8

a painted cupboard, trunk, or chest of drawers; the warm tone of wood easily fits in anywhere. The other shades in the room would simply have to be adjusted to the colours of the painted furniture.

A single piece of old furniture can lend to an otherwise somewhat neutral setting a very personal aura, a domestic atmosphere which is often lacking in our harshly prosaic houses. Pieces of old furniture, both rural and urban, are also well suited in their dimensions to our modern rooms, with their often modest proportions – much better than the sumptuous showpieces of antique furniture which were made for large, tall rooms.

Some of the illustrations show modern farmhouse rooms. The 'small farmhouse room' in the private house has little in common with the old farmhouse room. It serves as a place to eat between kitchen and living-room; it is not, as it was originally, the family's only living quarters.

The typical construction elements in the old farmhouse room – wooden ceiling, wood panelled walls, brightly scrubbed oaken tables in front of the corner bench – are readily adopted by hotels and inns, to offer a pleasant place in which to stay by providing a farmhouse atmosphere.

There are ideal examples, however, of the way in which the transference into a modern form-language can be successful, whether it be by means of a rough craftsman-like treatment of the wood, or by modern interior design methods such as the intensive use of colour effects.

A large proportion of the illustrations show modern country rooms. There seems to exist no relationship between them and farmhouse rooms, for these rustic rooms came about on an entirely different basis. In contrast to the farmhouse room, today's building methods make it possible to plan houses and rooms to whatever dimensions desired, and the new building materials are better suited to the construction of supporting ceilings than wood. Nevertheless a certain affinity with the former farmhouse room is sometimes discernible. One thing they have in common is the preference for wood as the raw material. Even if it is no longer structurally necessary, wood seldom represents simply a decorative element. A room in which a lot of wood has been used is of course warm and pleasant to live in. As a covering for ceilings and walls wood serves more than just as insulation and sound-proofing, for it also forms a very hard-wearing surface area. Wood is also suitable as a floor covering – simply as wooden boards, as parquet flooring like that of a ship, or as a particularly sturdy and durable wood-block covering.

Other traditional materials are to be found in the modern country-style room: floor coverings of natural stone (such as roughly hewn slate or quartzite), or fired bricks or slates, or of ceramic tiles – either brick tiles or tiles of the shape and type made for centuries (hexagonal or Florentine); also walls of unplastered or white scrubbed bricks, rough-cast or whitewashed.

But even quite modern materials need not look at all strange in a country room, as is shown by certain illustrations giving examples of concrete walls or ceilings.

Country-style rooms can be made in many different ways and in various materials. Common to them all is the renunciation of any attempt at pretentiousness, the restriction to simple and unextravagant forms and materials, to designs and craftsmanship which are functional and, not least, to what could be termed a homely and yet gracious atmosphere. This is achieved by a design which has remained the same from the centuries-old farmhouse room to the modern "little box" dwelling.

2 Tannheim valley room of the second half of the 18th century, showing a wall seat. There are elements of Rococo in the style of the painting. The bluey-green panels contrast with shades of reddish-brown.

3 Fireplace and antique utensils in a Tyrolean farmhouse.

4/5 Again a Tannheim valley room. The paintings are mainly in pale yellow and pink. From the time of the Rococo period there were permanent artistic centres in the rural areas of Swabia attracting the talent of folk artists. (Tannheim lies on the borders of Swabia and the Tyrol.)
The Tyrol Volks Art Museum at Innsbruck, with its many country-style rooms, is a treasure-house for all those interested in this rustic style and in folk art through the centuries.

11

6   A bedroom. Southern Tyrol. 17th century.

7   Renaissance room from the Tannheim valley, Southern Tyrol, in about 1612.

8   Room from the Upper Inn valley, 1692.

9   Gothic room in the Puster valley, Southern Tyrol.

10   Gothic room in the Eisak valley, Southern Tyrol.

11 Westphalia had its own styles in furniture and decoration in North Western Germany. Cupboards, chests, and seats were often ornately carved. Oak was the most widely used material.

12 A "milchschrank" made of oak, from the second half of the 18th century.

13 Living-room in a Lower Saxony farmhouse, featuring a plate-rack with household utensils.

14 Westphalian chest with rich symmetrical carving in oak.

15 Southern Tyrolean room in Baroque style, 1732.

16 Southern Tyrolean room in Gothic style. The leaf carving on the ornamental panels is an example of this particular creative country craft.

17 Swabian cupboard from a rural area. Originally it was probably painted. The curved cornice with carved overlaid motifs is typical of certain manufacturing towns such as Weissenhorn.

18 Low cupboard from the Ulm area. The ornamental devices were modified to a more rustic and primitive style. 1819.

19 The rural craft of furniture-making was deeply influenced by Rococo and still bears traces of it in the middle of the 19th century. This chest of drawers incorporates Rococo panels and a painted rose motif.

20 A four-poster bed, 1786. The headboard shows a painted biblical scene and the foot a basket of fruit. The borders have a motif of flowers and fruit, which together with biblical scenes are typical art motifs.

18

21   Country-style hotel bedroom in Upper Bavaria. In addition to single pieces one can sometimes see bedroom suites—i. e., a bed and a cupboard, or, as in this picture, beds and a chest of drawers, painted in the same style. There is even, in the Tolz Haus Museum, an early 19th century fitted wardrobe rather in the modern style, but painted in typical Tolz fashion.

22   Rustic cupboard from Tolz. "Blue and red are the farmer's favourite colours" was the saying, and it is not only true of Tolz rural painting. The effect of red roses is particularly good when they are highlighted in white against a dark blue background.

23 Modern living has re-discovered the delights of antique rural furniture. This shows a quaint four-poster bed and a painted cupboard in a Bavarian hotel room. The harmonising trimmings, such as the red check bed-spreads, the red curtains and chairs, create a very pleasing effect.

24 The clutter of furniture and effects here is perhaps reminiscent of the strange primitive pictures found in the bedroom of the painter Stefula.

25 In the Ulm area the Fussnet cupboard (of medium height) was very popular. This is a very pretty example, with panels in the Rococo style and an antique design in pastel colours.

26 Rococo-style chest of drawers (Zopfstil) in a style that is often found in Southern Germany. The feet are later additions.

27 Rustic cupboard, 1788, with ornate painting (Zillertal Alps).

28 A bed with unsophisticated painted design. The name of the owner is painted on it. Zillertal, 1788.

29 Cupboard from the Alps, 1770. In shape and design it is typical of primitive country craftsmanship.

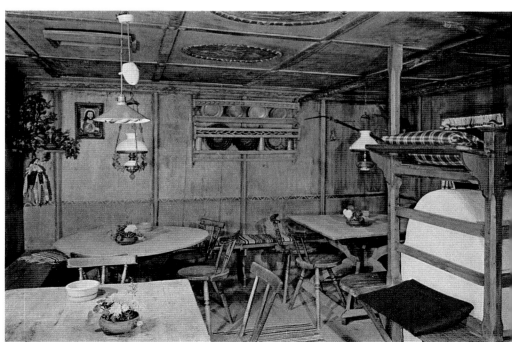

30 Country room from the Mindelheim area. It is panelled in wood and partly painted.

31 The stark white of the plaster and the dark grain of the wood make a pleasant contrast in this rustic interior. There is a sofa-seat lining the walls, an antique cottage table, and a red-tiled floor.

32 Swabian cupboards are usually carved and painted. This one, whose applied carvings are typical of the Weissenhorn district, is early 19th century.

33 Also from the Weissenhorn area, this chair is carved with Empire-style motifs.

34 Cupboard by Johann Michael Rössler, 1835. Rössler's furniture is unsurpassed by any in the 19th century. The simplicity of the cupboards is broken by Baroque-inspired flowers, figures, and fruit baskets.

35/36 Modern country room in Italy. The ceiling and walls are panelled in pine. The benches, table, and chairs are also made of wood. Wall shelves are a favourite decoration in rural areas and provide a convenient way of displaying antique pewter and other attractive antique or modern utensils. At the same time they are a way of adding individual character to a room.

37 Living-room in a farmhouse on Lake Garda. The heavy dark beams of the ceiling and round the open hearth, and the dark stained furniture, contrast well with the whitewashed walls. Check curtains highlight the quaint windows.

38 Much trouble has been taken in decorating this room to recreate the cosy atmosphere of country-style rooms of olden times. Traditional furnishings were used: a lot of dark stained wood, small windows, a massive table, and footstools.

39 Top section of a cupboard from Southern Tyrol with shelves for china. It is in natural carved wood.

40 The entrance hall of a Lombardy farmhouse. The fireplace is flanked by wall-seats and completely hooded with ancient stone.

41 Country dining-room in Italy. In spite of widespread poverty at the time, the tradition of a dining-table large enough to accommodate twelve people was current. On the mantelpiece are displayed ancient and modern household utensils.

42 Ancient cottage room from Wahrn near Brixen. Wooden benches are joined to the tiled stove.

43/44 Italian rooms in country style. The architect has tried to create the feeling of an old country setting by the use of gnarled pine with simple panelling, heavy wrought-iron fittings, and antique plates, etc.

31

45 Antique cupboard from North Italy. The piece has inserted painted panels and the style has elements of the Rococo. Roses and tulips are always favourite subjects in rural art.

46 Chest of drawers with elements of Gothic
style.

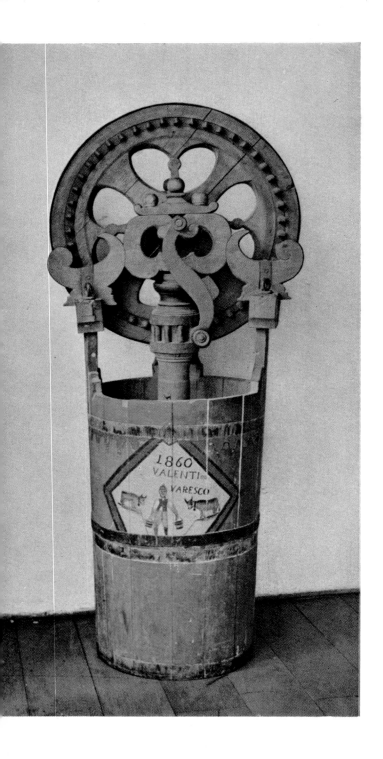

47 Elaborately carved butter-churn; the barrel is painted in primitive rural style.

48 Three-legged chair with rich ornamental carving.

49 Danish farmhouse interior. The chest dates back to the 17th century; it is decorated with ornate designs worked in iron, and the lock inside is perfect both artistically and technically. Above it is the front of a wainscoted chest (1828) with antique paintings.

50/51/52/53 Country villa. Only the same basic raw materials are used throughout the house, as, for example, the wooden spiral staircase in which each tread is inserted and pegged into the central newel post. Wood is used for the beams and ceiling as well as for the walls of the upper storey. The ground floor is brick-walled and the floor covered with Solnhofen tiles.

54 Ancient country room in a house in Tegernsee. The walls and floor are in wood. The small windows, typical of old farmhouses, give a feeling of comfort. There is a heavy antique table and armchairs in original rustic style.

55 Alcove seats in a wine-shop in the Tegernsee. The table is antique.

56 Living-room in Danish country house. The > high sloping ceiling is cut off visually by beams formed out of tree-trunks. The enormous round fireplace is in white plaster. The sofa is remodelled from an old chest. 1766.

57 Historical country rooms, like those in the wide selection of the Tyrol Volks Art Museum in Innsbruck, are excellent models when furnishing a modern room of this type, either for general style or for details of workmanship. The wooden bench, table, and the ceiling all show this solid craftsmanship. In the same room there are two antique chairs; part of an old choir stall completes the corner of the wall-seat.

58 Gothic room in Vintschgau (Southern Tyrol).

59 Room in a country house. The wall panelling
and table are in pine, and there is a tiled stove with
a ceramic chimney.

60 Gothic room from Southern Tyrol, with a bar-
rel-vaulted roof in wood.

61 One window in a Danish castle was glazed with frosted glass, and arranged as a display case for decorative antique bottles.

62 Room in rural Denmark; the furniture is late 19th century. There are painted panels, sometimes inlaid in wood.

63/64 Ornately carved antique salt-barrels from Northern Germany. About 1820.

65 This room in the Geffrye Museum, London, contains furniture of about the year 1600. The finely carved chests are typical of the period, the elaborate overmantel is from a larger house.

66 Armchair – so called 'box chair' – of oak, with the panels carved in relief with Renaissance ornament and linenfold. Second quarter of the 16th century.

67 Bedroom of the early seventeenth century, at Montacute House, Somerset. The bed frame is oak and the head-board is carved with the arms of King James I of England and of Frederick V, the Elector Palatine.

68 Turned oak chair, covered in leather, studded with brass-headed nails, in the puritan tradition of the mid-17th century in England.

69 Oak dresser, typical of many used in English country districts in the 18th and early 19th centuries.

70 'Windsor' armchair of carved and turned yew, in the 'gothick' taste of the mid-18th century.

71 Interior of the Red House at Bexley Heath, designed for William Morris by Philip Webb in 1860. This was the first country house to be built of brick for many years, and was a landmark in English domestic design.

72 Oak sideboard, carved and inlaid with ebony, sycamore, and bleached mahogany, designed by W. R. Lethaby about 1900. This piece is typical of the best work of the designers who continued the Arts and Crafts Movement which William Morris had inspired.

73 A room of the early 20th century in the Geffrye Museum. Wallpaper and curtains are William Morris designs; the furniture is by Voysey, Mackintosh, and Gimson, designers who revolted against the Victorian tradition.

74 Simple unit furniture adaptable to any room in the house, by Conran, 1969. The framework is steel, the panels and doors are surfaced in white lacquer.

75 In spite of its sparse furnishing this Belgian designer's living-room has an atmosphere of its own. The reddish wood ceiling has a slight polish and the floor gets its shape from the jointed ceramic tiles.

FROM DANISH HOUSES

76 The hall of this country house shows a light-coloured brick floor, whitewashed walls, and wood-boarded ceiling. The chairs show English influence in the carving of their backs. In fact, English, North German, and Danish pieces are quite closely related in general style. The heavy dark chest (1751) is only partly painted.

77 One could almost believe that the solid pieces of furniture have been standing for centuries in this country living-room with its tiny windows and wooden beams. The old paintings and the antique ornaments reinforce this overall impression.

78 Nature, in the form of a picturesque pond with water-lilies, becomes part of this room through the picture window. The old wooden chest with wrought-iron mountings contrasts with the more elegant chairs in Baroque style in front of the window.

79/80/81 The staircase is part of the living area in this one-family house in Stuttgart. It is given individual character by the choice of certain materials which are used consistently throughout the house: whitewashed walls, wooden ceilings constructed at different levels in dark and light panelling, and charcoal-coloured granite tiles on the floors. The stair support and the massive banister are made of layers of gnarled pine; the treads are carpeted.

82 Split-level living is an increasingly popular way of making the best possible use of available space. It creates a spacious and adaptable living area where there are pleasing effects of perspective. On the two upper levels dark wood pillars and panels contrast with a beige carpet and white doors. Downstairs the walls are covered in white plaster, contrasting with the dark parquet floor.

83 The idea behind the interior decoration of this house is to overcome its unfavourable position on a steep slope. The vast breadth of ceiling (beams and panels are of wood) covers the several levels of living space.

84   A Danish sculptor's studio. The wooden staircase leads from a split-level studio to the gallery
which is the working space (it is isolated visually
by surrealistic shapes). The walls are brick and the
ceiling is boarded in wood.

85   Living on several levels; steps lead from the
hall and adjoining dining area to the lower living
space and the garden. A spiral staircase of lacquered steel tubing with wooden treads leads to a large
living-room on the upper level. Ceiling beams and
wall panels are made of gnarled pine.

86 Staircases of light wooden construction do not narrow the room as they have a see-through effect. The staircase in a 'Knight's house' near the Castle of Solitude serves at the same time as a gallery for an exhibition of wall-clocks.

87 Some beautiful antique pieces lend individuality to this room where the steps lead to the next floor: a cupboard from the Lake Constance area, antique effects, paintings, and clocks.

88 The walls and ceiling of the living-room are completely panelled in wood. The dark stained wooden stairs lead to a gallery in the roof area of the house. The Bastiano armchairs with wide wooden frames by Padouk harmonise well with the range of dark to light shades shown in the wood.

89 The walls of this staircase, and the ceiling, are panelled in pine: the treads and banisters are of oak.

90 A plain rural staircase which is not too cumbersome in appearance. The gallery ceiling and walls are boarded with wood. The varying widths of the wood boards is an interesting feature. The stairs are carpeted.

PAGES 64 AND 65:

94 Collecting modern or antique objets d'art is a pleasant sideline to country-style living. Over the dining suite – a solid table and two single wooden benches – rows of framed pictures are attractively arranged.

95 Pottery from Vallauris (France), antique Bavarian beer mugs, brass candlesticks, and other examples of rural art concentrate the eye on the shelves above this inglenook. The walls and floor are red-tiled and the seats are made of white synthetic material with leather cushions. These are mass-produced pieces of furniture of excellent design.

96 Interior of a Provençal house. The massive ceiling beams and the quarry-stone walls make an attractive contrast with the delicate Persian carpets, dyed leaves and flowers, and modern ceramics.

91 Entrance hall of a photographer's house. The painted rural furniture from Southern Germany creates a homely atmosphere. There is no door between the living-room and the dining area.

92 The walls and ceiling of the hall are boarded in pine-wood. Inconspicuous wooden pegs, serving as clothes hooks, have been inserted into the boards.

93 The hall of this one-family house is wide and friendly, yet cosy at the same time. The effect of width is gained by the glass door and the light ash of the cupboard; that of cosiness is achieved by the irregular red tiles of the floor, the antique painted door of the built-in cupboard, the decorative fittings like the carved door-handle and the antique ornaments.

97 In spite of all the differences both rooms show one trend in common. There is a feeling of being in the security of a cave. This is achieved by the contrast of the chimney wall and the large living-room with its dark panelled walls and ceiling; it is emphasised by the leather cushions on their brick base and by the dark rough carpet made by Greek shepherds.

98 Sharp contrasts in the living-room of a house at Lake Como. The walls and ceiling are plastered red, and white ceramic tiles cover the floor and steps.

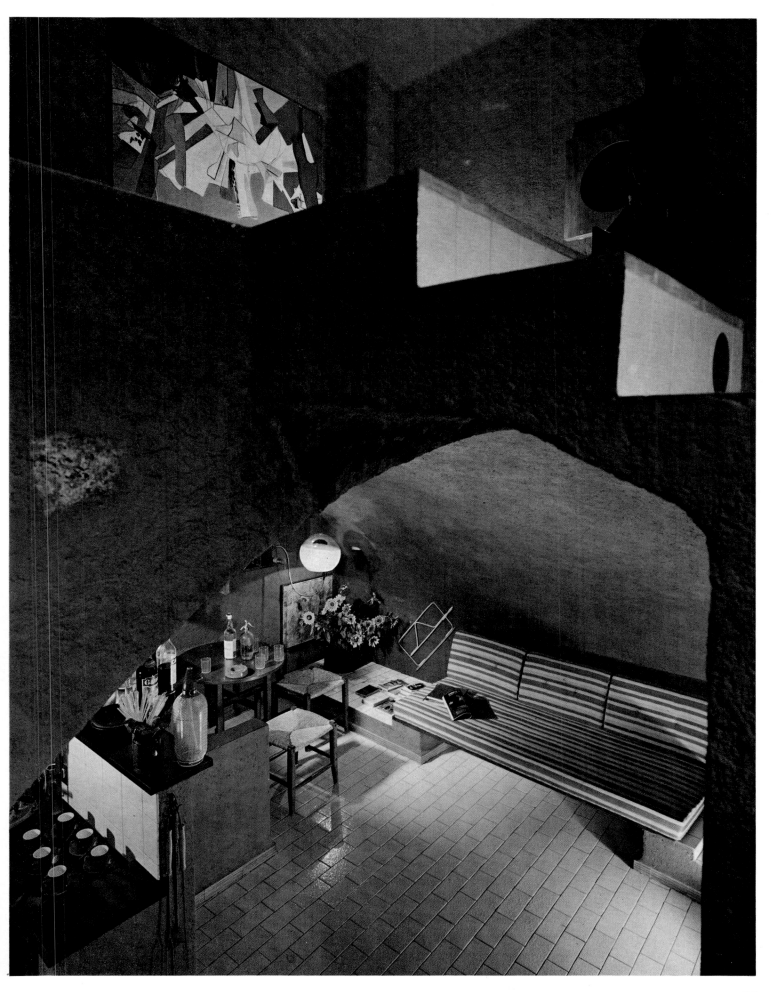

101 Attractive and practical combination of ceramic tiles and wood in a cellar. The ceiling and walls are of light pine. The curve of the wall, covered in blue ceramic tiles, forms a wall-seat and the hearth of an open fireplace. The grate and flue are made of black lacquered cast-iron.

99/100 Modern living in an Eifel hunting lodge. The particular atmosphere of the room is achieved by the use of contrasting materials; the walls are of quarry-stone, the floors are tiled, and wood is used for the ceilings, joists, and window-frames. There is a hatch into the dining area. The dining table and chairs are of teak and the seats are of black leather.

102 Living-room in an Eifel hunting lodge. The enormous fireplace is built of quarry-stone. An interesting feature is the way the unusual shape of the ceiling is joined to the window wall.

103 A country living-room in Italy. The fireplace
with its round white-plastered cowl is of the most
basic form.

104 Artist's studio in Italy. Wooden stairs lead to
the living space in the gallery. The floor is covered
in red tile. The artist's own tools and storage chests
are supplemented by historical painting implements.

105 In this Italian living-room the open fireplace is built like a block of concrete. The patterned tiled floor and two box settees set off the visual effect of the fireplace.

106 A country house in Italy. The old wooden ceiling, the large fireplace, and the white plaster flue make the room seem warm and cosy. The red and white lacquered seats are points of interest in this room.

107 Living-room of a country house in Italy. Heavy red and white lacquered seats with cushions covered in tartan material contrast with the dark wood of the ceiling and the black wood block floor.

108 Cocktail bar in the hall of a Florentine villa. This centuries-old room with its irregular wooden ceiling and Florentine tiled floor is an impressive setting when guests gather at the bar. They sit on small barrels in front of an enormous wine-barrel which has been converted into a bar-counter.

109 In this Italian house a barrel serves as a bar, and there are quaint footstools and several interesting bar accessories.

110 Country dining-room. The construction of the wooden ceiling can be seen. Comfortable wicker chairs surround the table and copper pans and engravings decorate the walls.

111 The vast fireplace wall contains two hearths; one heats the living-room, the other (of which only the flue can be seen) heats the bedroom. Unsophisticated materials such as brick and wood are used. In this Italian seaside house the living area is sparsely furnished.

112 Dining area in the hall of an Italian house. It is floored with ceramic tiles and the wall is partly built of quarry-stone. Chairs from the Ticino area are made of poplar wood; these are also popular in Germany.

113/114 In this room the whitewashed brick fireplace has a look of plastic. There is an attractive play of forms in perspective, with alcoves, flat surfaces, and projections. The fireplace can be seen as well from behind the chimney wall as from the living-room. The floor is stone, and the joists and ceiling are of wood.

115 This is reminiscent of traditional fireplaces in country houses. The beams supporting the white plastered hood of the hearth are themselves supported by heavy iron rods and chains. The ceiling is of dark stained wood, and the floor is covered with ceramic tiles.

116 A modern tiled stove in white plastic with a black frame divides the living-room from the ante-room where it can be stoked. The whole of this farmhouse attic is carpeted throughout and the wood ceiling, boarded in pine, gives a feeling of space to the rather small rooms.

PAGES 80 AND 81:

117/118 The charms of living right under the roof have been re-discovered in modern times. Nowadays the shape of the roof is exploited in the interior decoration, whereas the tendency before was to hide the angles of its construction. The height of the gable, boarded in pine, creates a feeling of space. However, the dark stained joists give limits to the room, and one never feels lost there, despite the high roof. The wicker chairs are suspended on chains from the ceiling beams.

119 Here it is the interesting metal construction below the pine-boarded gable that is the essential element in the room's design.

120 The same idea. The roof is boarded with wood and supported by metal joists. The walls are panelled in pine and a frameless skylight has been let into the pediment of the roof.

121 The half-timbered style is maintained throughout this house. The gable which we see is trimmed
with spruce.

122 The roof of this country house is also boarded
with pine. The unconcealed roof framework splits
up the large living area and at the same time forms
the kitchen space which continues through to the
dining area.

123 Wood is again the main material in this country house in Weisenburg near Vienna. The ceiling
joists are of wood, and there are veneered sheets
on wall and ceiling. The window and door frames
are of wood, and, last but not least, there is Danish
furniture in wood; Denmark has been producing
these folding chairs for more than thirty years.

124/125 Here an old farmhouse with a large roof projection has been converted into a holiday home on the banks of a Swiss lake. Older touches, such as the ceiling made of thick oak, have been carefully preserved or highlighted; modern ideas like the picture window, the open fireplace, the wall panelling in wood, and the wood block floor have been skilfully incorporated into the design.

126 The living-room of an architect's house. Only
a few materials are used throughout the house. The
ceiling is made of concrete as are the bookshelves
on the whitewashed brick wall. The floor is made
of red brick, and the same material is used for the
heating strip inserted in front of the large sliding
windows. The grate of the open fireplace is also
brick. The decor is entirely functional, and every
sort of ornamentation is dispensed with.

127/128 A farmhouse in Heidelberg. The beams visible both inside and out are stained red. In place of curtains there are red lacquered sliding doors at the french windows. One of the doors is painted with abstract designs, also in shades of red. The whole idea of this house is reminiscent of an old farmhouse with a large threshing floor. Bedrooms, studies, nurseries, and kitchen lead off from both sides of the living-room, which has a gallery above the dining area.

129 A modern frame house in Heidelberg. The beams are stained red and they form a screen which divides the room. The open fireplace is made of sheet iron lacquered black.

130 This fireplace shows the artist's love of graphic decoration. The mantelpiece and hearth are partly tiled with a geometric pattern. The flue is made of sheet iron and lacquered black.

91

131 All these different objects illustrate the various interests of the inhabitants of this architect's house. There are modern paintings and plastics, ancient Asian puppets, and Oriental carpets. The architect himself designed the simple furniture. Their massive dimensions counterbalance the other elements in the room which have rather a light effect.

132 Even contrasting elements can make a harmonious whole in modern interior decoration. Here there is a rural cupboard from Ottobeuren painted in earthy colours, an English naval chest in mahogany, a Horst Antes painting, an Italian chandelier, and pine ceiling and walls. All these different elements, ingeniously arranged by the designer, are an excellent illustration of 'harmonious country living'.

133 Glazed red ceramic tiles cover the whole of
the floor of this house at Lake Como. Beside the
door leading to the terrace overlooking the lake
there is an alcove which has a cave effect because
of its lowered ceiling. The two settees, covered in
red material, may also be used as beds.

134 A modern suite of chairs of rustic design, in dark-stained natural wood.

135 The Italians have a different and more positive attitude to colour than our own. The living-room and gallery of this house at Lake Como has a colour scheme which incorporates red ceramic floors, white walls, dark stained wood in the gallery, banisters, and fireplace, and red seats and upholstery.

136 Multi-level living: the wooden framework of the rooms forms an attractive meeting point for the vertical and horizontal elements of the room. The ceiling and walls are panelled in the same material. The upper-level dining area is carpeted, while the living area is of natural stone.

137 The rural setting invades this room through the vast picture windows. The boarded gable roof extends over the terrace, the whole of which can be seen from the window.

138 Concrete, one of the modern building materials, may also be used in the context of 'country
living'. The ceiling above the generous curve of the
fireplace is made of concrete and the floor is of
inlaid pebbles. Loose leather cushions on built-up
wooden bases, serve as seats.

139/140 The fireplace and wall are made of concrete. They contrast with a sloping pine ceiling and
dark wood frame windows.

141/142 This split-level living area displays many aspects of modern design. The chimney corner, with its low ceiling, gives a feeling of cosiness. The dining area with the central grouping of chairs is hidden from the living-room. The brick walls are whitewashed and the remaining walls, ceiling, and the balustrade are wood-boarded. The floor is covered in baked clay tiles. All these points emphasise the rural atmosphere of the room.

143 This elegant chimney corner has been achieved by the use of basic materials. The Marini lithograph, in shades of bright red, stands out against the stark white of the brick wall.

144 Dining area in a hall. The Scandinavian dining suite is in teak and the ceiling is boarded in pine wood. Fabric blinds on a wooden rod replace curtains.

145 A cavalier's house near the Castle of Solitude near Stuttgart has been converted into a family house. The rural character of this small house and its affinity with the garden is emphasised by the wood ceiling, and the wickerwork chairs. There are many fine examples of traditional rural craftsmanship.

146 This room shows wooden furniture placed right in front of a wood-panelled wall – an antique walnut writing-desk and modern bookshelves in light wood. This idea works successfully because of the way the different woods harmonise. In front of the wood-panelled wall stands a modern bookshelf. The homely dark surroundings make an especially good contrast with the light wood.

147 Living in the attic. The roof gable has been > boarded with light pine, and the heavy joists serve a joint decorative and structural purpose.

148 This living-room's individual character comes from the interesting ceiling construction. The warm texture of wall and ceiling coverings, such as the wooden beams, the wood panelling on the far wall, and the brick chimney breast, contrast with the cool, light stone floor. All these elements form a neutral setting for the antique cupboards and chairs.

149 Living-room in a converted millhouse. The central fireplace has an old gear-wheel as firebed. The bare brick walls and floor are softened by the use of rugs and hangings.

150 This staircase is built in a very confined area, but achieves a feeling of spaciousness by the large window overlooking the millstream.

151 Steel framed chair, with latex foam upholstery, 1969.

152 This rural dining-room has 19th century
chairs, an oil lamp, and home-made pine shelving
filled with a collection of interesting crockery and
stuffed birds.

153 All the rooms in this lake-side house show rural influences. The cloakroom is separated from the hall by a heavy linen curtain. The heavy ceiling beams are another interesting feature.

154 There is a feeling of space in this country-house cloakroom. This is achieved by the use of the same materials there as in the adjoining hall – wood-boarded ceiling and walls, quarry-stone on one wall, and red clay tile flooring. Two plexi-glass skylights, as well as concealed lighting behind a wooden screen, provide good natural and artificial light above the two washbasins.

155 Attic bedroom in an Italian farmhouse. A light wrought-iron staircase leads to another bedroom where the beds are in curtained alcoves. In the larger room massive dark furniture and the heavy beams contrast with the whitewashed walls and the fragile staircase.

156 Attic bedroom. In this lake-side house the walls and floor are boarded with pine. The beautifully constructed wooden staircase is a decorative addition to the attic.

157 An attic bedroom in a converted lake-side farmhouse. The charm of the room lies in the contrast between the massive wooden beams and boards, and the stippled white plaster and the pink tiled floor. Beneath the gallery there are two divan beds; simple wooden shelves replace the more traditional bedside tables.

158 In this oak-beamed bedroom the architect designed a mahogany bed. The frame is laid on four heavy posts, and at the bedhead a bookshelf is built into the frame. The designer has taken advantage of the steep angle of the roof by building a walk-in wardrobe.

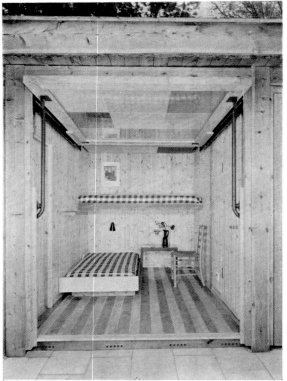

159 In this children's room the wall behind the bunk beds is panelled in pine. The high window can be covered in by a blind of the same material.

160 You can walk on to the terrace of this country house from its nursery when the glass door slides up into the ceiling. The walls are wood-panelled and the tile flooring in wood is hard-wearing and warm. It is the ideal material for this purpose.

161   The ceiling, walls, and floor of this skiing hut in Italy are boarded in wood. The room has a warm, cosy, but at the same time unsophisticated atmosphere.

162   The slight inward slope of the wall gives the room a cosy atmosphere which is further emphasised by the wooden wall, the triangular shelving, and the wrought-iron work on the trunk.

163 This bedroom has a somewhat spartan appearance. There is a wooden block floor, white walls, wicker chair, and a mahogany folding table. Only the deep colour of the bed brings some life into the room.

164 The deeply panelled Frankfurt cupboard in walnut blends here with the heavily beamed ceiling.

165 Rural colour scheme in a kitchen. The white working surfaces, red check curtains, and deep red cooking utensils make a pleasant contrast with the dark green fittings.

166 A small storeroom next to the kitchen is completely tiled in green ceramic. In the alcove the shelves are of dark wood.

167 A kitchen which is too neutral can be given atmosphere by coloured chairs, pretty patterned curtains, and attractive accessories. In this kitchen there are various types of baskets hanging from the ceiling.

168 Farmhouse-style kitchen in a prefabricated house. The dark ceiling beams, panelled walls and ceiling, and light-weight kitchen furniture combine to give a countrified effect.

169   This open-plan room has a great feeling of spaciousness, but the living and dining areas are well defined. This view is looking past the dining area to the garden, beyond the seating area. (Left)

170   The view from the other side of the openplan living area shown in 169. Light-coloured woods add to the feeling of space. (Above)

171   Kitchen unit built in whitewashed bricks, with a dark stone plate. As well as the hotplates, a barbecue is incorporated into the surface of the range, and there is a steam flue above it. A sliding door separates the kitchen from the dining area. The floor is covered with dark slabs of slate.

172 The kitchen of a country house in Salzburg. The floor is wood block, the walls and working surfaces are tiled, and the kitchen cupboards are of wood. One clever feature is the way the garden dining area leads out from the kitchen.

173 This kitchen is furnished with mass-produced pieces of rural design in dark wood. The steam flue above the kitchen unit is of copper, and the unit itself is tiled with a patterned design.

174 Even an ultra-efficient kitchen may be a winner > for looks. A ventilation screen is incorporated into the wooden ceiling. The rather hard look of the moulded plastic units is softened by scattered coloured ornaments.

175   The whitewashed brick work, the red tiled floor, and the massive wooden furniture create a unique atmosphere in this old house.

176   The brick kitchen shelves act as a room-divider in this kitchen-living area. An essential factor in any plan which puts a cooking and a living area in such close proximity is perfect ventilation – in this case an enormous flue in the kitchen. The ceiling is made of wood, and the furniture is also of wood. This is from a Danish house.

177/178 The path from the living-room to the garden seat in the overgrown garden is very charming. Thick trunks surround the seat. The dining area in the house is shaded by a blind suspended from the over-hanging roof.

179 The garden of Vienna architect Professor Roland Rainer's house. The artistically built stonework forms the framework of the garden, and the group of seats and sparse natural growth complete the picture.

180 Study place in the garden of a sculptor's studio. Antique glass globes from country gardens blend with the work of modern sculptors.

181 Modern design caters for both inside and outside rooms. This garden living area is part of the house. The fireplace would be a popular focus for conversation on warm summer days. The brickwork of the room is whitewashed and the ceiling and part of the walls are panelled in wood. The floor is made of concrete.

182 This roofed porch is screened from a small kitchen courtyard. The bricks are whitewashed and the ceiling and part of the walls are wood-panelled.

183/184 A covered bench and dining area. There is a barbecue with a copper smoke flue. The dividing wall, in dark wood with a screen effect, has a decorative purpose as well as a practical one, of storage.

185/186 A loggia added to a mountain home. The overhanging roof, and the wood panelling on walls, ceiling, and floor create a sense of security in this 'outdoor' living area.

187/188 There are charming contrasts in this house at Lake Como. The cavern effect of the living-room is emphasised by the deep red plaster. The beautiful setting, sea and mountains, penetrates the room through the large picture windows.

189 Patio on the ground floor of a house at San
Filice Circeo. The brickwork is plastered in white,
and dark beams and raffia form a protection
against the sun. In spite of these rural elements, it
is the elegant sea-green tiled floor which dominates.